TRIBES of NATIVE AMERICA

Choctaw

edited by Marla Felkins Ryan
and Linda Schmittroth

BLACKBIRCH®
PRESS

THOMSON
— ✦ —
GALE

San Diego • Detroit • New York • San Francisco • Cleveland
New Haven, Conn. • Waterville, Maine • London • Munich

Photo credits: Cover Courtesy of Northwestern University Library; cover © National Archives; cover © Photospin; cover © Perry Jasper Photography; cover © Picturequest; cover © Seattle Post-Intelligencer Collection, Museum of History & Industry; cover, pages 3, 25 © Blackbirch Press Archives; cover © Library of Congress; cover © PhotoDisc; pages 5, 6, 22, 23 © Marilyn "Angel" Wynn, nativestock.com; page 12 © Sun Valley Photography, nativestock.com; pages 7, 18, 20, 30 © AP Wide World; pages 8, 13, 29 © Library of Congress; pages 8, 23, 24, 31 © CORBIS; page 9 © Courtesy of Colorado Historical Society, CHS-J-1450, photo by W.H. Jackson; pages 11, 28, 31 © Hulton Archive; page 16 © Dancing Rabbit Resort; page 17 © Corel Corporation

LIBRARY OF CONGRESS CATALOGING-IN-PUBLICATION DATA

Choctaw / Marla Felkins Ryan, book editor ; Linda Schmittroth, book editor.
    v. cm. — (Tribes of Native America)
Includes bibliographical references and index.
Contents: Choctaw name — Origins and group affiliations — History — A painful journey — Common Choctaw expressions — Economy — Daily life — Customs — Education — Current tribal issues.
  ISBN 1-56711-688-4 (alk. paper)
  1. Choctaw Indians—Juvenile literature. [1. Choctaw Indians. 2. Indians of North America—Southern States.] I. Ryan, Marla Felkins. II. Schmittroth, Linda. III. Series.

E99.C8 .C456 2003
976.004'973—dc21   2002015822

Table of Contents

· FIRST LOOK ·

CHOCTAW

Name

The Choctaw (pronounced *CHOCK-taw*) called themselves the Chataogla or Chata.

Choctaw
Contemporary Communities

1. Choctaw Nation of Oklahoma
2. Mississippi Band of Choctaw Indians

Shaded area: Traditional lands of the Choctaw in east-central Mississippi

Where are the traditional Choctaw lands?

The Choctaw originally lived in Mississippi in villages like this one.

The Choctaw first lived in what is now the southeastern United States, mainly in Mississippi. Today, there are large Choctaw communities in southeast Oklahoma and Mississippi. There are also smaller ones in Louisiana and Alabama.

What has happened to the population?

There were about 20,000 Choctaw before the Europeans came. In a 1990 population count by the U.S. Census Bureau, 82,299 people said they were Choctaw.

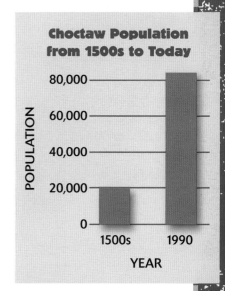

Choctaw Population from 1500s to Today

Origins and group ties

The Choctaw homeland is in east-central Mississippi. In the 1830s, most of the tribe moved to land west of the Mississippi River. Some people think many of the native groups of the southeastern United States were once Choctaw.

The Great Seal of the Choctaw Nation of Oklahoma was adopted in 1860.

The Choctaw were a peaceful people. They would defend themselves if they were challenged, but they did not often start wars against other tribes. At one time, the Choctaw lived on more than 23 million acres in Mississippi and parts of Alabama and Louisiana. The Choctaw were forced to move to Oklahoma in the 1830s. The people now live on two main reservations in Oklahoma and in Mississippi.

Choctaw Tully Choate performs a traditional dance during a festival in Kingman, Arizona.

HISTORY

A Choctaw legend says that long ago, a Choctaw leader named Chata led his people on a trip. He had a sacred pole that he stuck in the ground at the end of each day's journey. Each morning, the pole leaned to the east. The people moved on, and crossed the Mississippi River. One morning, when they woke up, they saw that the pole stood up straight. At that spot, they buried the remains of their ancestors to form a sacred mound.

According to legend, a mound similar to this one was formed where the Choctaw buried their ancestors' remains.

In the 1500s, the Choctaw fought with Spanish explorers led by Hernando de Soto (center).

Spanish explorer Hernando de Soto was the first European known to meet the Choctaw. De Soto and members of his party came to Choctaw lands in the 1540s. De Soto demanded that the Choctaw give him women, as well as people to carry the Spaniards' bags. A fight broke out. Choctaw losses were heavy, but many Spanish were wounded, too. After the battle, the Spaniards crossed Choctaw land without any more contact.

Relations with the French and Americans

In the early 18th century, English slave raiders from the Carolinas made thousands of Choctaw slaves. The French started their colony of

1830
The Treaty of Dancing Rabbit Creek is signed. It forces the Choctaw to move to lands west of the Mississippi River

1861
American Civil War begins

1865
Civil War ends

1914–1918
WWI fought in Europe

1918
The Bureau of Indian Affairs sets up the Choctaw Indian Agency.

1929
Stock market crash begins the Great Depression

1941
Bombing at Pearl Harbor forces United States into WWII

1945
WWII ends.

1975
Choctaw national offices are set up

1983
The 1860 Choctaw Constitution is ratified. It gives the Choctaw Nation of Oklahoma the right to govern itself

Louisiana in 1700. At first, the Choctaw got along with the French. But in the 1730s, the French wiped out the Natchez, a nearby tribe. The Choctaw took in the survivors. They became suspicious of the French.

A Choctaw civil war took place from 1747 to 1750. It was fought between tribal members who wanted to keep trade relations with the French and those who wanted to trade with the English instead. The war was so severe that it wiped out entire villages and greatly weakened the Choctaw.

During the American Revolution (1775-1783), the Choctaw sided with the Americans. They made their first treaty of friendship with the Americans in 1786. When a second treaty was signed in 1801, Americans began to settle in Choctaw country in large numbers. In 1805, Americans began to pressure the Choctaw to move west of the Mississippi River. Even so, the Choctaw stayed loyal to the United States.

In 1811, the tribe forced Shawnee leader Tecumseh to leave their lands when he tried to get the Choctaw to join an alliance against the United States. The Choctaw then fought against the Creek in a war that began when the Creek joined Tecumseh's alliance. The Choctaw also helped U.S. general Andrew Jackson's army fight the British. Despite all this, in 1816, the United States demanded that the Choctaw give up a great deal of their land.

A painful journey

By 1820, many of the Choctaw had agreed to give up some of their lands and move west of the Mississippi River. About 6,000 chose instead to stay on the more than 10 million acres of original homeland they still held east of the Mississippi. In 1830, under the Treaty of Dancing Rabbit Creek, the Choctaw were forced to give up those eastern lands and move as a full tribe to the West. This move took place from 1831 to 1834. It was part of a larger forced Indian move from the Southeast. The move came to be known as the Trail of Tears because of the terrible suffering the native peoples

This painting shows a Choctaw camp along the Mississippi River in the 1800s.

went through. On their trip to Indian Territory (land that now forms most of the state of Oklahoma), many Choctaw faced starvation and bitter cold. Nearly half of the tribe died on the way.

The promise

Cherokee (pictured) and Choctaw were among the Native American tribes who were forced to move west from their homelands in the east. This journey became known as the Trail of Tears.

The Treaty of Dancing Rabbit Creek made the Choctaw give up their lands, but it also made a promise to them. It said that the United States would always let the Choctaw govern themselves and would never try to take over their new lands.

During the mid-1850s, the Choctaw in the West were able to build a strong economy. They also started a public school system and made laws to govern themselves.

INDIAN LAND FOR SALE

GET A HOME

OF

YOUR OWN

✻

EASY PAYMENTS

PERFECT TITLE

✻

POSSESSION

WITHIN

THIRTY DAYS

FINE LANDS IN THE WEST

| IRRIGATED IRRIGABLE | GRAZING | AGRICULTURAL DRY FARMING |

IN 1910 THE DEPARTMENT OF THE INTERIOR SOLD UNDER SEALED BIDS ALLOTTED INDIAN LAND AS FOLLOWS:

Location.	Acres.	Average Price per Acre.	Location.	Acres.	Average Price per Acre.
Colorado	5,211.21	$7.27	Oklahoma	34,664.00	$19.14
Idaho	17,013.00	24.85	Oregon	1,020.00	15.43
Kansas	1,684.50	33.45	South Dakota	120,445.00	16.53
Montana	11,034.00	9.86	Washington	4,879.00	41.37
Nebraska	5,641.00	36.65	Wisconsin	1,069.00	17.00
North Dakota	22,610.70	9.93	Wyoming	865.00	20.64

FOR THE YEAR 1911 IT IS ESTIMATED THAT 350,000 ACRES WILL BE OFFERED FOR SALE

For information as to the character of the land write for booklet, "INDIAN LANDS FOR SALE," to the Superintendent U. S. Indian School at any one of the following places:

CALIFORNIA: Hoopa. COLORADO: Ignacio. IDAHO: Lapwai. KANSAS: Horton. Nadeau.	MINNESOTA: Onigum. MONTANA: Crow Agency. NEBRASKA: Macy. Santee. Winnebago.	NORTH DAKOTA: Fort Totten. Fort Yates. OKLAHOMA: Anadarko. Cantonment. Colony. Darlington. Muskogee. Pawnee.	OKLAHOMA Con. Sac and Fox Agency. Shawnee. Wyandotte. OREGON: Klamath Agency. Pendleton. Roseburg. Siletz.	SOUTH DAKOTA: Cheyenne Agency. Crow Creek. Greenwood. Lower Brule. Pine Ridge. Rosebud. Sisseton.	WASHINGTON: Fort Simcoe. Fort Spokane. Tekoa. Tulalip. WISCONSIN: Oneida.

WALTER L. FISHER,
Secretary of the Interior.

ROBERT G. VALENTINE,
Commissioner of Indian Affairs.

The U.S. government used posters like this one to advertise Native American land for sale in the West. The Choctaw was one of many tribes who were forced to give up land for white settlement.

Choctaw resettle in Oklahoma

The Choctaw sided with the southern states during the American Civil War (1861-1865). Afterward, the U.S. government forced the Choctaw to sell their western lands. The tribe signed a treaty in 1866 that gave railroad companies the right to build tracks across Choctaw lands. More white settlers came to live near the new railroad. By 1890, Americans on Choctaw land outnumbered tribal members by three to one.

Around 1900, the Choctaw and other tribes were forced to move to a different place in the rapidly changing region. Each nation had to divide its land into individual pieces called allotments. They could no longer own the land as a tribe, as they had always done. By 1907, when Oklahoma was made a state, the Choctaw tribe was dissolved. Its members had to become citizens of the new state.

At first, the Choctaw language and culture did well after the tribe moved to Oklahoma. But an outbreak of influenza (an illness that was often fatal back then) during World War I (1914-1918) killed 20 percent of the Oklahoma Choctaw. The allotment policy was also a disaster for the tribe. Within one generation, most of the allotted land had been sold to whites, often through trickery.

The Mississippi Choctaw

Though most of the Choctaw were forced to move west, about 6,000 stayed in Mississippi. Almost all of these Choctaw lost everything they owned. They became squatters on the land that had been their own. Many eventually moved west to join the rest of the tribe.

In 1918, the Bureau of Indian Affairs opened the Choctaw Indian Agency in Philadelphia, Mississippi. The agency set up schools in poor Choctaw communities. It also gave the tribe financial aid. During the early 20th century, the boll weevil (a type of beetle that kills cotton plants) infested crops in east-central Mississippi. This took a severe toll on the economy of the region. The Choctaw there faced terrible hardship. In the second half of the 20th century, good tribal leadership helped make economic conditions of Choctaw in both the East and West better.

This 1937 photo shows young Choctaw women learning traditional crafts at an Indian arts and crafts center in Oklahoma.

Choctaw today

During the 1970s, Choctaw chief Hollis Roberts worked to get back the Choctaw Nation's right to govern itself. In 1975, Choctaw tribal offices were set up in Durant, Oklahoma. In 1981, the U.S. government recognized the 1860 Choctaw Constitution. It was ratified (approved) by the Choctaw people in 1983. Today, the Choctaw Nation of Oklahoma runs programs in areas such as health and housing for its 80,000 people. Money earned from tourist attractions helps the tribe improve their living conditions.

The Choctaw earn money from tourist attractions, such as the Dancing Rabbit Golf Course in Mississippi.

Religion

The Choctaw did not worship a single supreme being. They saw the sun as a very powerful force. Tribal members often got advice from people, such as healers and rainmakers, who were said to have special powers. Medicine men were expected to predict future events. These people were also said to make warriors brave and a hunt successful.

The sun was a powerful force in the Choctaw religion.

The Choctaw believed that two kinds of souls lived on after a person died. The first soul frightened living people or took on the form of an animal. The second was an inner spirit. It began its trip to the afterworld right after death.

The afterworld had two sections, one good and one bad. People could end up in the bad section if they murdered someone or told lies that led another person to commit murder. A person who gossiped or divorced a pregnant wife could also be sent to the bad section.

Government

The Choctaw tribe had many subgroups, or bands. The oldest man in each band, the ogla, was the chief. The ogla shared his wisdom with the rest of the tribe and helped teach the people. He also played a big role in ceremonies.

Today, the government of the Oklahoma Choctaw is run by a tribal council. It is made up of a chief and 12 members. The Mississippi Choctaw Reservation is run by a 16-member council. The chief serves for 4 years. He runs council meetings, which take place 4 times a year.

In March 2002, Chief Phillip Martin of the Mississippi Band of Choctaw Indians (right) attended a ceremony at the site of a tribal construction project.

CHOCTAW POPULATION: 1990 CENSUS

The U.S. census said there were 82,299 Choctaw in the United States. Of these, 26,884 lived in Oklahoma. The Mississippi Band of Choctaw reported 9,050 Choctaw in its band in 1995. Choctaw identified themselves this way:

Tribe	Population
Choctaw	65,321
Mississippi Choctaw	2,624
Mowa Band of Choctaw, Alabama	947
Oklahoma Choctaw	17,323
Other Choctaw	16

Economy

For centuries, Choctaw people grew crops on the river floodplains where they lived. The tribe held their land in common. Individuals could, however, claim a field if they could farm it and if they did not interfere with fields already claimed by others. If a person abandoned a field, the tribe took back control over it.

Today, many Choctaw work in the tourism industry. Bingo has helped the major Choctaw tribes earn a lot of money. The Oklahoma Choctaw

Nation's Choctaw Bingo Palace draws busloads of bingo players each day. The Mississippi Choctaw tribe's Silver Star Casino makes about $100 million a year. Other businesses also employ Mississippi tribal members. Many Choctaw work in manufacturing and agriculture. Others run an industrial park.

The Oklahoma Choctaw have a fishing plant and a shopping center. They also have travel plazas and a health center. The Choctaw Nation also publishes a tribal newspaper called *Bishinik*. More than 1,400 people work for the tribal government. In fact, the government provides more jobs than any other employer.

In the mid-1990s, per capita income on the Oklahoma reservation was very low–about $6,200. (Per capita income is the average amount one person earns in a year.) The level of income for the rest of the United States was about $20,000.

DAILY LIFE

Families

Girls were brought up by their mothers. Sons were brought up by their mothers' brothers. These uncles were the closest of the boy's male relatives within his clan. Clans are groups of related families. They were the basic unit of Choctaw society.

Choctaw men wore loincloths. Men and women both wore face paint and brightly colored feathers.

Buildings

The Choctaw lived in lodges shaped like circles. The frames were made of sticks, and palmetto thatches covered the tops and sides. Each lodge had one door. It usually faced south. There was an open fire in the middle of the lodge. An opening in the roof let out smoke. Many people lived in each lodge.

Choctaw homes were round and had one door that faced south.

Clothing

Choctaw men wore belts and loincloths. In the winter, they added moccasins, leggings, and garments made of feathers or mulberry bark. Women wore short deerskin skirts. In cold weather, they also wore deerskin shawls and moccasins. The Choctaw wore earrings and feathers of bright colors. Both men and women wore face paint and tattoos. Men wore their hair long, with bangs and braids. Women wrapped their long hair into a roll at the back of their heads.

Food

The Choctaw hunted many animals, including bear and turkey. They also caught trout and shrimp. These were eaten fresh or dried to be eaten later.

The Choctaw also gathered berries that were eaten fresh. Grapes and crabapples were dried. The main crops grown were squash and corn.

Education

In early times, Choctaw boys and girls learned to use blowguns to hunt small game. The blowguns were pieces of cane, about 7 feet long. They blew sharp cane darts. Before the tribe had guns, Choctaw children were taught to hunt larger game with bows and arrows. They also learned to catch fish with traps.

From the mid- to late-1800s, the Oklahoma Choctaw had a successful school system. When the Choctaw Nation was abolished in 1907, though, the Choctaw became citizens of Oklahoma. Their school system ended.

The U.S. government started schools for the Mississippi Choctaw in the 1920s. Still, education for the average Mississippi Choctaw is poor. Casino profits have helped the Mississippi Choctaw start a school. It gives classes in Choctaw language, history, and arts.

Top: The Choctaw used blowguns and darts to hunt small animals. Bottom: A student receives a history lesson at a Choctaw school in Mississippi.

Healing practices

The Choctaw treated diseases with herbs and other plants. Sometimes, medicine men also helped cure people. They boiled roots to make medicines. They washed wounds and treated snakebites. They also treated fever and helped fend off smallpox.

The Choctaw wrapped themselves in several layers of cloth and drank hot tea to sweat disease out of their bodies. To cure stomach pains and arthritis, they put a small compress on the place that hurt. They treated broken bones with wraps and splints.

Arts

Choctaw music stresses that it is important to live in harmony with nature. Most Choctaw dances took

A Choctaw man performs a traditional dance.

Basket weaving is an art among Choctaw women.

place in an open field. They were done to the beat of drums and sticks. Three major dances are still done. Animal dances are held to honor birds and animals. The Green Corn Dance, held in late summer, looks forward to the corn harvest. Both men and women take part in the Choctaw war dance. In past centuries, it took place for eight days before a battle. A chanter, often a young man, leads the songs for dances. He starts with a shout, then the other dancers join in.

Choctaw swamp cane baskets are highly valued. Basketry skills are usually passed down through families. Choctaw women use unique beadwork designs that feature scrolls and other very old Choctaw designs.

CUSTOMS

Festivals

Traditionally, the Choctaw did not have fancy ceremonies. Today, though, they host one of the top American Indian events in the Southeast. This is July's Choctaw Fair, held in Philadelphia, Mississippi. The fair features tribal ceremonies and dances. Ethnic foods are served and stickball games are played. There is also a craft fair. Another event is Oklahoma's Annual Choctaw Festival. It draws nearly 10,000 visitors.

Every year in Skullyville, Oklahoma, on the first Saturday in June, members of the Choctaw tribe meet to remember the forced move of their people to the West. The thousands of Choctaw people who suffered and died in the early 1830s during the journey are honored. A symbolic reenactment of the walk is done. The people also eat traditional foods and do tribal dances.

Speech-making

The Choctaw were very good public speakers. When a formal debate was to take place, a large shelter was built with a hole in the center of the roof. Those who wished to speak stood under the hole in the

The Choctaw host festivals each year where traditional dances are performed.

heat of the sun. The audience sat comfortably in the shade. The idea was that audience members could bear to listen as long as the speaker could stand in the heat and speak.

Games

Recreation was very important. Ishtaboli, a form of stickball, was (and still is) a favorite sport. It was sometimes used to settle disputes. A leather ball was slung from a webbed pocket at the end of a long stick toward the opponent's goal at the end of the

This illustration shows Choctaw men playing ishtaboli, a form of stickball. The sport is still popular among Choctaw today.

playing field. The games were rough. Sometimes, serious injury or even death resulted.

Courting and marriage

When a young man found himself alone with the woman he loved, he would move close to her and toss a pebble. If she smiled, it meant she approved of the courtship. If she disapproved, she gave him a scornful look. Another way to court a young woman was for a man to enter her lodge and lay his hat or handkerchief on her bed. If she approved, she let the item stay on the bed. If she disapproved, she took it off the bed. If they both agreed to the union, they set a time and place for the wedding.

During a wedding, the couple's families stood about 100 yards from one another. The bride's brothers went to the groom and seated him on a blanket. The man's sisters went to the woman and did the same. The woman's family put a bag of bread near her. The man's family set a bag of meat next to him. Friends and relatives of the man then showered gifts over the head of the woman. The gifts often included clothing and household items. The couple then rose together and everyone went to a feast.

Death

The Choctaw believed that the soul was immortal. The spirit of the dead person was thought to stay near the corpse for a while after death. In ancient times, the body was wrapped in skins and bark. It was then placed on a platform with food and drink nearby. After a few days, it was the job of certain people who had long fingernails to take the rotting flesh off the bones of the dead person. The bones were then given to grieving relatives. They painted the skull red and placed it in a coffin.

A modern-day Choctaw family poses for a picture in Chucalissa, Tennessee.

In more recent years, a deceased Choctaw was dressed in special clothing so the community could view the body. The clothes were not buried with the person. Often, a hunter's gun was placed with him in his grave. Mourning periods were based on the age of the deceased.

In 1999, Chief Gregory Pyle of the Choctaw Nation of Oklahoma spoke to a Senate committee about issues affecting Native Americans.

Current tribal issues

The two largest Choctaw groups—the Choctaw Nation of Oklahoma and the Mississippi Band of Choctaw—are recognized by the federal government. Other Choctaw groups, though, such as the Mowa Choctaw of Alabama, still seek federal recognition.

The Mississippi Choctaw have been able to get businesses to come to the reservation, since an industrial park was built in 1973. Large corporations there employ about 1,000 Choctaw. The Oklahoma Choctaw have also begun successful tribal businesses. Bingo has made the tribes on both reservations the most money.

Both the Mississippi and Oklahoma Choctaw have set up housing authorities. These have helped the reservations create affordable modern housing.

Notable people

Pushmataha (1764–1824) was a Choctaw warrior, statesman, and chief. He was loyal to the United States and would not join an Indian confederacy against whites.

Rosella Hightower (1920–), a world-famous ballerina, has also directed ballet and opera companies.

Educator Linda Lomahaftewa (1947–) is a painter whose works highlight the culture of the Plains Indians.

Choctaw chief Phillip Martin (1926–) worked to help the Choctaw economy grow.

Chief Hollis E. Roberts (1943–) fought for his people to become a self-governing nation.

For More Information

Choctaw Vision, homepage of the Mississippi Band of Choctaw.

http://www.choctaw.org

The Choctaw Nation of Oklahoma homepage.

http://www.choctawnation.com

Top: Pushmataha
Bottom: Rosella Hightower

Lepthien, Emilie U. *The Choctaw.* Chicago: Childrens Press, 1987.

McKee, Jesse O. *The Choctaw.* New York: Chelsea House, 1989.

Glossary

Allotments individual pieces of land

Raid an attack on land or a settlement, usually to steal food and other goods

Reservation land set aside and given to Native Americans

Ritual something that is custom or done in a certain way

Treaty an agreement

Tribe a group of people who live together in a community

Index

Allotments, 14
American Civil War, the, 13
American Revolution, the, 10
Animal dances, 25

Bands, 18
Baskets, 25
Bingo, 19–20, 30
Blowguns, 23
Boll weevil, 15
Bureau of Indian Affairs, 15

Chata, 8
Chataogla, 4
Choctaw civil war, 10
Choctaw tribal seal, the, 6
Clans, 21
Creek, the, 10

de Soto, Hernando, 9

Influenza, 14

Ishtaboli, 27–28

Jackson, Andrew, 10

Lodges, 22, 28

Natchez, 10

Railroad, 13–14
Roberts, Chief Hollis, 16, 31

Sacred mound, 8
Sacred pole, 8
Slaves, 9
Souls, 17, 29

Tecumseh, 10
Trail of Tears, 11–12
Treaty of Dancing Rabbit Creek, 11, 12

U.S. Census Bureau, 5, 19